MIRACLES AND DIVINE PROTECTION

MIRACLES AND DIVINE PROTECTION

ACCOUNTS OF ANSWERED PRAYER

SALLY MONDAY

RISE UP
PUBLICATIONS

Released June 2024

ISBN: 978-1-64457-736-3

Rise UP Publications
644 Shrewsbury Commons Ave
Ste 249
Shrewsbury PA 17361
United States of America
www.riseUPpublications.com
Phone: 866-846-5123

DEDICATION

I gratefully dedicate this book to my mother, Helen Shannon, who raised me to know and love Jesus, Father God, and the Holy Spirit. She taught me how to press into God and lean on Him in childhood and adulthood. She was not only a great caring mother in the natural but amazing in the supernatural as well.

Mother taught me how to apply the Word to prayer and get answers. We agreed in prayer throughout my entire life. People were miraculously healed and set free; all glory be to God. She taught me to expect the divine intervention of God in my life and in others.
Yes, she taught me what quality of life was, to be respectful, to pursue excellence in all aspects of life, and to be successful as to honor God with everything I had and would be.

Although she lived a full blessed life here for ninety-seven years, she left me with the greatest treasure of a lifetime. Knowing how to seek God first and all of His righteousness. Showing me the ways to live in His presence and depend solely upon Him.

She was the praying mother that everyone wished they had. Always faithful to God, His Word, prayer, and fasting. I am only here today because of her prayers for me that saved my life. The Holy Spirit would wake her up to pray if I was in danger. God's angels have rescued me from death because she prayed. I hope to pass that on to my four children, whom I also raised in a Christian home. She left me an invaluable legacy that I hope to pass on and share with others.

But Jesus beheld them, and said unto them,
With men this is impossible; but with God all
things are possible.

CONTENTS

INTRODUCTION

Many people have told me that I should write a book about my life because I have had so many of God's interventions save, heal, and deliver me even from death. I finally have time to write my stories after retiring from teaching, and my children are all grown and on their own. God deserves all the credit for what He has done to save, heal, deliver, and restore me and my family.

In obedience to the Word, I am sharing my testimonies of how I have walked in the wondrous miracles of God and His supernatural protection. You will read about the acts of God according these quotes of Jesus, found in the books of Acts and John. What the enemy meant for evil, God turns around for good.

"But you will receive power and ability
    when the Holy Spirit comes upon
    you; you will be My witnesses[to tell
    people about Me] both in Jerusalem
    and in all Judah, and Samaria, and
    even to the ends of the earth."

— ACTS 1:8 (AMP)

"Amen, amen I tell you, he who puts his
    trust in Me, the works that I do he
    will do; and greater than these he
    will do because I am going to the
    Father.
And whatever you ask in My name, that
    I will do, so that the Father may be
    glorified in the Son.
If you ask Me anything in My name, I
    will do it."

— JOHN 14:12-14 (TLV)

The Bible also tells us that the same power that raised Christ from the dead dwells in us today as it did in Him. With these accounts of God's interventions and miracle encounters in this book, you will be introduced to who God is. He is the Father of the fatherless, the Teacher, Healer, Savior, Deliverer, Way Maker, Prince of Peace, and Almighty God.

According to Ephesians, we are predestined, therefore God is the actual author of my life's miracle stories rather than I. Never would I blame God for any of my troubles. I only give Him glory, honor, and praise because He has delivered me out of all the enemy's plans to destroy me and my family.

> In Him we also were chosen, predes-
> tined according to His plan. He
> keeps working out all things
> according to the purpose of His will–
>
> — EPHESIANS 1:11 (TLV)

In God's plan for my walk with Him, He instantly healed my injured knee, He straightened and grew my leg with a creative miracle, and He popped my hip back into place after not being able to walk for two weeks. I was able to walk again all because of prayers that God heard and answered.

You will see that when praying with a sincere heart, God will guide and direct you. He will give His angels charge over you, help you in times of trouble, and deliver you from the evil plans of the enemy who intends to steal, kill, and destroy lives. You will learn that if God can save and protect my life and the lives of my family, He too will save and protect you and your family.

Unlike Joyce Meyer's life story about years of continued abuse from her father with a mother who failed to protect her from him, I was the mother who said, "Absolutely not on my watch!" You will see how my mindset went into the protection mode of a mama bear. God sent me help from the police, Child Protection Services, Harborview Medical Center, angels, the court system, an attorney, my family, and Christian people.

God gave us new names, a way of escape, and protection from my children's abusive father who attempted to kidnap them at different times. Although I had a restraining order, God kept us hidden from those hired to follow us for many years and from the stigma that follows children who are sexually abused by a father.

It was 30 years of hiding until the abuser passed away five years ago. Still, I am cautious about naming names because I never want to go back to the high-level stress of monthly and, sometimes, weekly court motions and hearings filed by my ex-in-laws. Still, my mind is programmed to stay hidden, telling my stories in the third person. I always thank God, that He gave us a fresh new start and divine protection.

By God, I am enabled to do acts of love, forgiveness, healing, and miracles in Jesus' name because I know Him, and because I am baptized with the Holy Spirit and power. This is the common thread to hearing God's voice and seeing Him intervene which anyone can choose to pursue.

> "For John baptized with water, but you
>   will be baptized and empowered
>   and united with the Holy Spirit, not
>   long from now."

— ACTS 1:5 (AMP)

Nothing on this earth compares to experiencing God's presence combined with His miracles and answers to prayer. It is key to know Jesus and dwell in God's presence through meditation on His Word and prayer in the Holy Spirit.

God promises in His Word, that what He has done for others He will also do for you. As you read these miracle encounters, expect that God will help you in your circumstances as well. No matter what your situation is, He is waiting for you to call out to Him so that He may answer your petitions and show you great and mighty things as you will see He has done for me.

We just must do our part to ask, seek, and knock so He can do the rest to answer, reveal, and open doors of miracles to us. I thank our great and mighty God in advance for the miracles you are about to receive in your life as you take hold of the Scriptures included at the end of each of these accounts. Apply these verses by praying them aloud for the situations or trials you are experiencing.

CHAPTER 1
DADDY GOD REVEALED

There was a little girl, Sally who received Jesus into her heart on her knees beside her mother during family devotions. Her mother recalls her as being two years old at the time she asked Jesus to forgive her sins and to be the Lord and Savior of her life. Although she did not have a dad in her life, her mother explained that God in heaven was the Father of the fatherless. The little girl learned to believe in the Bible and saw answers to prayer from an early age.

When Sally started kindergarten, she went to her first school assembly. The special guest was a TV show host named Brakeman Bill. He dressed like a train conductor, and he was known to draw famous cartoon characters. Everyone who came to the assembly got a raffle ticket. Brakeman Bill explained that he would draw some pictures and then call the ticket number for the winner of the picture.

Brakeman Bill began drawing a huge picture on a large easel for everyone to see. Little Sally thought to herself, I can pray to my Daddy God so that I am the winner of the picture. So, she prayed, "Dear God, please let me be the winner of the drawing. I am Your daughter in Your kingdom, and I should have the picture because I am Yours." Brakeman Bill completed the jumbo-sized drawing of the famous Snoopy as if he were doing a happy dance. It was so cute!

The winning ticket was pulled out of a bucket, and the numbers were read aloud to the auditorium. The kindergartener Sally had the winning ticket even though she needed help to read its numbers. She jumped up and was told to come up front to get her Snoopy Dog picture. Brakeman Bill rolled up the drawing, put a rubber band around it, and congratulated her for winning the prize. She went back to her seat with the Snoopy drawing, knowing that her Daddy God cared about her winning it, which meant He really loved her as His child.

Sally shared how God answered her prayer with her older brother on the way home from school. He asked if he could have the Snoopy drawing. She gave it to him without hesitation because she was more overjoyed and thankful that her Daddy God heard and answered her prayer, than being the winner of the drawing itself.

At a young age, Sally valued the knowledge of her heavenly Father hearing and answering her prayer. She strongly felt God's presence and love toward her, so how could the object of the prize itself compare to having a Father God who is the Father of the fatherless, as her mother had taught her from the Bible?

> A father of the fatherless and a judge
>   and protector of the widows is God
>   in His holy habitation.
>
> — PSALM 68:5 (AMP)

> Every good thing given and every
>   perfect gift is from above; it comes
>   down from the Father of lights, [the
>   Creator and Sustainer of the heav-
>   ens], in whom there is no variation
>   [no rising or setting] or shadow cast
>   by His turning [for He is perfect and
>   never changes].
>
> — JAMES 1:17 (AMP)

> 'Call to Me and I will answer you, and
>   tell you [and even show you] great

and mighty things, [things which
have been confined and hidden],
which you do not know and understand and cannot distinguish.'

— JEREMIAH 33:3 (AMP)

When God answers our prayers, it is the absolute depiction of the Snoopy Dog drawing. He is smiling and jumping around doing the "Happy Dance," just like King David who danced with joy before the Lord in the Bible. What is more exciting than getting answers to prayers?

CHAPTER 2
LEARNING MIRACLES

The little girl Sally had learning issues. She was unable to read even though she knew her letters and sounds. It was apparent she needed special reading instruction. She was unable to read like the other students and was falling behind in other subjects as well.

Sally struggled to copy her math problems correctly too. If she copied a math problem, it did not match the math book. By the time she entered 2nd grade, she had learned some self-coping skills to read numbers aloud, double-check the order, and leave spaces between to squeeze in numbers that were omitted or transposed. She also learned to track letters with her finger and to make the sounds of letters in order: to blend the sounds, say the words slowly, and reread them for meaning.

When her mother moved her to a Christian school, Sally was able to get extra help learning to read and start developing reading skills; it has been a lifelong strategy for her to learn. By the time she was finishing high school, Sally considered going to college because she would receive benefits due to her dad's death as a full-time student. Although reading was still a struggle, she enrolled in community college.

Sally's main interests were the Arts and Interior Design. She chose the Interior Design program that was offered and managed to complete the two years of community college. It took her four times as long to study and comprehend the material as it did other students. To understand her college textbooks, she had to decode words, reread sentences aloud, highlight topics in different colors, and diagram her study notes.

Sally knew it would be more of a challenge to go to a university, but she wanted to complete a bachelor's degree in fine arts, as she was already halfway there. After enrolling at Seattle Pacific University, she went to an orientation meeting.

Of course, at the meeting, she sat in the front row to focus, take notes, and understand what the expectations were to obtain the 4-year degree. Within the first few minutes, she realized she was in the wrong meeting because it was all about education and teaching. However, she was too embarrassed to walk out.

Suddenly, she felt like there was a hand pressing on her right shoulder and she knew there was no one there. It must have been an angel. In her spirit, she heard a voice saying, "No, you are in the right place; stay and take notes." So that is what she did.

Looking through the SPU classes catalog that evening, Sally wanted to transfer her two years of credits from her Interior Design Program. She wrote out three separate lists of courses needed for three different bachelor's degrees. Fine Arts, Art–Education, and Fine and Performing Arts were the most compatible choices which she listed on three different yellow tablets.

Knowing God created her, she knew that God could direct her to choose the best path. So, she prayed that God would show her the best choice. Faithfully God answered her by giving her a repeating vision. During her waking moments, she saw herself in a vision, rolling up the Art-Education tablet with its list of courses, and then eating it. Even though every time she tried to go back to sleep, she could not. She saw the same vision again three times.

Finally, Sally went to ask her mother why she would have this vision three times. Her mother asked her, "What have you been praying about?" She explained she wanted to know what direction to go with her bachelor's program. Then Sally knew God was answering. Her mother explained that three is the number of the Trinity of God and how there was a prophet in the Bible who did the same thing by rolling up the scrolls and then eating them.

The young lady realized the hand of God was directing her even when she thought she had gone to the wrong orientation. It turns out she was in the right place, and she got her answer to prayer. She decided to pursue her B.A. in Arts and Education. It was a miracle that with God's help, she graduated from SPU with a bachelor's degree in visual arts and became a teacher.

She began her career teaching third grade in Christian schools. Now she can even read upside down while teaching her students across from her with their books facing toward them. She has also developed her own instructional technique to write cursive letters in reverse in the air, "Skywriting," to observe students tracking their hands with hers. She teaches students how to form numbers and letters in manuscript or cursive from her right to her left in reverse.

After teaching third grade for ten years at the Crystal Cathedral Academy, she decided to enroll in a Master of Education program at Azusa Pacific University. When taking the required instructional course for teaching disabled students, she discovered that she had struggled with dyslexia. She learned that most women are never diagnosed because they usually can develop coping skills and just deal with it. No doubt she fits into that category.

It is a miracle that she earned straight A's in her master's program, and she gives God all the glory. She realized it was a miracle that she ever became a teacher. Her struggles were turned into strengths as God helped her each step of the way. She helped students who were struggling as she had. God caused her inadequacies and weaknesses to become advantages that benefited her instructional methods. God helped her do what seemed impossible!

Sally took different teaching positions available for Art, unlike earlier in her career. She developed lessons for grades K-8. God inspired her to adapt her instructional strategies to the language arts steps of writing. Students learned to pre-sketch, plan color schemes, practice drawing techniques, and edit their work before creating a final work of art.

Students learned to critique their own artwork by reviewing the project objectives with a partner to check if they fulfilled their goals. Students used Sally's teacher-created Rubrics to score their artwork with a buddy for accountability. Then the students handed in their critiqued artwork with their scored Rubrics. These Rubrics became learning tools for students to not only review project objectives and develop critiquing skills but also identify any missing components that could be added to their piece or edited from their artwork as it also contributed to building the Art community.

The Art teacher used her God-given strategies and methods for teaching Art combined with her class-room teaching experience. Sally designed student projects that met state standards and created artwork examples that were step-by-step and heartfelt. Students were given every possible opportunity to succeed in Art class.

Sally coordinated Annual Art shows that included the Music and Band program in presentations of artwork from ages 5–13. Families who attended enjoyed their children's talents and appreciated the students' amazing artwork displayed. These were some of Sally's best years of her career while teaching Art.

> But seek ye first the kingdom of God,
> and his righteousness; and all these
> things shall be added unto you.
>
> — MATTHEW 6:33

> In all thy ways acknowledge him, and he
> shall direct thy path
>
> — PROVERBS 3:6

Thy Word is a lamp unto my feet, and a
    light unto my path.

— PSALM 119:105

God faithfully directs our paths when we desire His perfect will and plan for our lives. It is up to us to pray and pursue what He has designed us to be and for what purpose. Prayer is the best way to find and experience true fulfillment in life. Ways that God enables us, His children, to carry out His perfect plan for our lives are through divine providences working in our lives, the counsel of caring Godly people that lines up with His written Word.

CHAPTER 3
FIELD TRIP INJURY

While attending a Christian grammar school in 4th grade, Sally went on a field trip with her classmates. She was running and did not see the branch of a tree that she ran straight into; her open eye took the impact. She was in pain, and her principal on the field trip called her mother. Her mother left work and drove to the park location.

The injury looked bad, so her mother drove her to the ER. Sally and her mother prayed in the Spirit on the way. When they parked the car, they prayed in English. The mother reminded her that God is the Father of the fatherless and the Bible says, "Ask anything in Jesus' name and agree as touching anything, I will do it." They prayed in agreement in Jesus' name that the pain would be gone and her eye would be healed.

Sally had been holding her hand over her injured eye closed on the way to the hospital. Now parked in the parking lot, the pain was gone. She flipped down the visor to look in the mirror and surprisingly all the red was gone, and her eye was completely healed. It was a healing miracle!

Together they praised God, her Father in heaven, and decided to go home, joyfully thanking Him all the way. There was no injured tissue, no redness to show a doctor, and no pain!

> Again I say unto you, That if two of you
> shall agree on earth as touching
> anything that they shall ask, it shall
> be done for them of my Father
> which is in heaven.
> For where two or three are gathered
> together in my name, there I am in
> the midst of them.
>
> — MATTHEW 18:19-20

> If ye shall ask any thing in my name, I
> will do it.
>
> — JOHN 14:14

Every good gift and every perfect gift is
from above, and cometh down from
the Father of lights, with whom is no
variableness, neither shadow of
turning.

— JAMES 1:17

Thus saith the Lord, the Holy One of
Israel, and his Maker, Ask me of
things to come concerning my sons,
and concerning the work of my
hands command ye me.

— ISAIAH 45:11

For verily I say unto you, That whoso-
ever shall say unto this mountain, Be
thou removed, and be thou cast into
the sea; and shall not doubt in his
heart, but shall believe that those
things which he saith shall come to
pass; he shall have whatsoever he
saith.

— MARK 11:23

Halleluiah! Over and over, God proves His Word to be
true. When we pray aloud together and remind God of

His promises to us, we speak the Word to activate miracles through faith. We can mix our faith by praying the Scriptures, standing in truth, believing, and not doubting in our hearts so that God will perform His Word by whatsoever we speak. Isn't it amazing that we can speak healing if we only believe and not doubt?

CHAPTER 4
SKI TRIP INJURY

At twelve years old, Sally started to take skiing lessons on the weekend. In Washington State, the snow in the Cascades can be plentiful, but if it is not very cold, the snow gets heavy like oatmeal, making it hard to turn one's skis. Toward the end of the day, after a ski lesson, she took a turn in the heavy snow. The resistance caused her to fall, injuring her knee.

The ski patrol came and removed her skis and put her on a toboggan. She was examined at the Ski Patrol office, and they put her leg into a cardboard splint. She was carried onto her ski school bus to be taken home. When her mother took her to the doctor, it was discovered she had torn the cartilage in her right knee. The doctor said that the only way to fix the injury was to have surgery.

Sally was full of faith, being raised in a Christian home where there were nightly devotions of prayers, sharing Bible story lessons, and discussion time. Her family was in church every time the doors were open, every Wednesday evening, Fridays for special speakers, Sunday mornings, and Sunday evenings.

Philadelphia Church, in Seattle, is where she and her family attended. They would commonly open the basement for the people who wanted to stay and pray after services. It would get loud down there with a roar of tongues, and miracles were known to occur. Sometimes, there was corporate prayer time agreement and the gift of tongues and interpretation operating too.

Pastor Johnson was very careful to only have visiting speakers who moved in the Holy Spirit. One Sunday evening, a speaker was operating in the gift of faith and healing miracles. At the end of his message, the special speaker opened the altar to those who wanted prayer for healing.

On her crutches, Sally hobbled her way to the front of the church. As he began to pray for her, she felt heat come into her knee area and it began to tingle. Joy filled her heart as tears began to roll down her cheeks. God was touching her with His love and healing her injury. The speaker asked her to walk without the crutches. She said yes, knowing her Father God is also the great physician and that He healed her.

It was a miracle! She went walking back and forth with no pain, jumping up and down with no pain, and leaping and praising God! Crutches were no longer needed, and surgery was no longer needed either! All she could do was rejoice in the Lord and know how wonderful it is to have God as her Father. She knows the goodness and faithfulness of God who is the Healer!

> With men it is impossible, but not with God: for with God all things are possible.
>
> — MARK 10:27

> Thou hast beset me behind and before, and laid thine hand upon me.
>
> — PSALM 139:5

> I will praise thee; for I am fearfully and wonderfully made: marvelous are thy works; and that my soul knoweth right well.
>
> — PSALM 139:14

> And he took him by the right hand, and lifted him up: and immediately his

> feet and ankle bones received
> strength.
> And he leaping up stood, and walked,
> and entered with them into the
> temple, walking, and leaping, and
> praising God.

— ACTS 3:7-8

During her college days, Sally became a strong skier who trained to race in downhill giant slalom racing. She competed against men because no other women were training. God blessed her with great strength in her legs. All glory to God, she even earned Physical Education credits toward her bachelor's degree.

According to Jesus, it is lawful to do miracles every day or wherever we are inside or outside of the church. Jesus came to save, heal, deliver, and fulfill the law even on the Sabbath. We serve a loving God with wonder-working healing power. God's works are marvelous yesterday, today, and forever. He always changes lives for the better through His abundant love and tender mercies. Hallelujah!

CHAPTER 5
CREATIVE MIRACLE

At age 16, Sally attended a Sunday evening church service at Harvest Time Church. Her family heard of miracle meetings happening there. After the meeting, the lady speaker came over and asked her if she could check the length of her legs. Because she responded yes, the lady asked her to sit tall and straight, all the way back into her chair.

Next, the lady asked her to lift her heels up, and as she held them in her hands, it was evident that the right leg was about two inches shorter than the left one. It was also noticeable that the right leg shin bone was bowed out and appeared somewhat crooked. Sally's mother said that her foot was turned in at birth, although it seemed to have straightened out as she got older to walk as a toddler.

The lady began to pray and speak to the bone to grow and to straighten in Jesus' name. Sally could feel stretching as she saw the bone lengthened and watched as the shin bone moved into a straightened position. As the lady prayed, the right leg began to change to match the left leg. The lady asked God to make her legs perfectly straight and to be equal lengths. As it happened, she continued to hold Sally's outstretched legs by her heels.

Father God's love was poured out through her as Sally received her creative miracle in her right leg. Her family watched and shared in seeing the miraculous experience. It appeared like God was sculpting the flesh and bone of Sally's leg as if it were clay in His invisible hands.

The joy of the Lord was so prevalent in her. She wanted to tell everyone what the Lord had done for her. That Sunday night, she asked her mother to go to her cousin's home nearby. They went to tell her auntie and cousin's family what had happened. Once there, she walked, ran, and jumped around their house praising God, proclaiming the miracle that she had the perfect walk and perfect legs.

> And he saith unto them, Is it lawful to
> do good on the sabbath days, or to
> do evil? To save life, or to kill? But
> they held their peace.

he saith unto the man, Stretch forth
thine hand. And he stretched it out:
and his hand was restored whole as
the other.

— MARK 3:4-5

Who his own self bare our sins in his
own body on the tree, that we, being
dead to sins, should live unto righteousness: by whose stripes ye were
healed.

— 1 PETER 2:24

Bless the Lord, O my soul, and forget
not all his benefits:
Who forgiveth all thine iniquities; who
healeth all thy diseases;

— PSALM 103:2-3

And whatsoever ye shall ask in my
name, that will I do, that the Father
may be glorified in the Son. If ye
shall ask any thing in my name, I
will do it.

— JOHN 14:13-14

And he took him by the right hand, and
lifted him up: and immediately his
feet and ankle bones received
strength.
And he leaping up stood, and walked,
and entered with them into the
temple, walking, and leaping, and
praising God.

— ACTS 3:7-8

It is wonderful to experience God's creative miracles by simply stretching out one's limb in obedience to what God wants to do. We can expect miracles in His presence. Jesus healed in the synagogue on the Sabbath in the house of God and still does today.

Twice, Sally had a miracle in her right leg during a Sunday evening church service. This shows that attending church on Sunday evenings is important if you want a miracle. During Bible times and nowadays, God is the same loving Father. What a marvelous healing, faithful, and loving God we serve!

The miracle was that she stretched forth her legs to become the same length and that she too received perfectly straight legs. Her joy was evident through her walking, jumping, and running around with excitement. Not only would she walk, run, jump, and ski differently in the natural world, but she would also walk, run, jump, and ski differently in the Spirit realm because this experience affected her ability, strength, performance, and life forever.

CHAPTER 6
TEEN HOME MEETING

S ally and her brother were on their way home after an evening youth group home meeting. Her older brother in high school was driving, and they were talking about how God had done so many miracles that night during the gathering. The gifts of the Spirit were operating, and people were getting saved, filled with the Spirit, healed, and delivered.

One boy was brought to the meeting by some Christian friends. Her brother saw in the Spirit: Write letters across his forehead that said "bondage." He told the Lord I need more than that. Then he heard the word "coke."

In the hallway, he prayed for the boy to be loosed from cocaine and drugs. The boy jerked back flat against the wall. He slid down the wall unnaturally and slithered along the wall and out the door. Later, they found out from his friends that he went to church the next Sunday, gave his life to God, and got delivered from drugs.

However, while they were driving home from the meeting, her brother began to tell her that he had a word of knowledge for someone else. He said he missed the opportunity to share it at the home group meeting because it was over, and people had gone home.

She asked him what that word of knowledge was about. He told her that God showed him a lump in a woman's breast. He knew that God would have healed her too, because God only shows us the issue if He is going to fix it or heal it.

Sally's response was, oh my goodness, that's me. I have been praying about the ping pong ball-sized lump in my breast, it has been bothering me, and I have been concerned about it. I thought I would have to tell Mom and make a doctor's appointment to get examined.

Surprised, he immediately said, I know God's going to heal you. He began to pray and thank God it wasn't too late for the opportunity to heal, but right on time. They continued to pray in the Spirit while driving home.

He asked God in Jesus's name that He would dissolve the lump. When his sister Sally checked it, God had shrunk the lump to the size of a pea. He then took authority over that lump and commanded it to go, and he rebuked it from her body. They spoke in tongues together and in agreement in the name of Jesus.

Once they were home, they told their mother the miracles God had done. Then Sally checked for the lump again when she was home, and it was completely gone! God knew the right timing and place for the opportunity to pray and see His healing power during the car ride home with the right person there. They all rejoiced in the faithfulness of God.

> And whatsoever ye shall ask in my
> name, that will I do, that the Father
> may be glorified in the Son. If ye
> shall ask any thing in my name, I
> will do it.

— JOHN 14:13-14

> But Jesus beheld them, and said unto
> them, With men this is impossible;
> but with God all things are possible.

— MATTHEW 19:26

> For verily I say unto you, That whoso-
> ever shall say unto this mountain, Be

thou removed, and be thou cast into the sea; and shall not doubt in his heart, but shall believe that those things which he saith shall come to pass; he shall have whatsoever he saith.

— MARK 11:23

What an amazing God we serve! He is faithful not only to showing us the needs of others but also to meeting those needs of salvation, healing, and deliverance as well. Glory to God!

It is a matter of speaking to the problem. Sally's brother spoke to the lump in her breast to be removed and dissolved and it was gone, according to the spoken Word of God in Mark. What an everlasting gift and treasure of life to be raised by a mother who taught them to know and act on the Word of God and to pray and get results. All things are possible for those who believe!

CHAPTER 7
GOING TO CALIFORNIA

At 19 years old, a young lady decided to go stay with her sister in Inglewood, CA, which is close to Venice and Santa Monica Beaches. Her sister was having surgery and school was out for the summer. What a good reason to go to California, to be helpful!

The young lady met a young man at Santa Monica Beach. He introduced himself as Rodney, a professional photographer and a graduate of UCLA. Her passion was also in the arts. She was planning to attend community college for two years and then possibly go to Seattle Pacific University. Rodney was an impressive six foot, five inches tall, dark, handsome, and friendly kind of guy. He asked the young lady out on a date with him to visit and tour the campus of UCLA. She answered yes to the invite which sounded intriguing.

He picked her up in his little orange Fiat, and they toured around the campus. He was friendly with professors and people who knew him in the UCLA community stopped to talk with them.

When her older sister came home from the hospital, they had Rodney over for dinner. Afterward, her older sister told her that something about him seemed strange and creepy, and she advised her younger sister not to have anything to do with him. Although he had already gotten her home address in Seattle, she figured she would not have to respond to his letters. She did not want any encounters with a strange and creepy guy.

Sure enough, when she got back home, he wrote her letters about coming to visit and spend time with her in Seattle. She did not respond to Rodney as her older sister had advised, sensing that he was odd and should stay away from creepers. She never wrote him back or had any contact with him ever again.

Thirty years later, the young lady's photo, as well as those of 130 other girls, were published on the Nancy Grace Show with the question, "Have you seen these girls?" The same young lady, who was now in her 40s, received a call from her mother, saying she saw her picture on TV and called her to find out if that was her. She denied it could be her because she did not want her mother to worry.

It turns out Rodney Alcala was tagged with the title 'Dating Game' killer who was convicted of killing at least seven women and attempted to kill an 8-year-old girl in LA. He was known to torture, strangle, rape, and kill his victims.

In 1986, there was a retrial for the murders of five girls in California that he had previously gotten off for due to technicalities, but this time he was convicted and given the death penalty. Again, this was overturned in 2001, so he got out and continued killing women. Finally, in 2010, he was convicted by his DNA of semen and sentenced to death for the third time.

Praying mothers make a difference. Yes, some of the photos were of his victims, but not the one young woman who had a praying mother. Thank God for the protective angels assigned to this young lady whose mother was praying for her safety! What the enemy meant for evil, God intervened, and that young lady made it home alive to tell her story.

Never communicating with Rodney after meeting him in 1977 in California, she left Seattle in 1988 and changed her name. It was a huge surprise that the detective found this young lady in 2012 in Arizona. He said that he had been trying to locate her for thirty years.

Thirty years later, she spoke with a Seattle Police Detective who flew to Arizona to interview her. He informed her that Rodney Alcala used her name and address to rent a storage unit in Seattle, where he stored over 1,000 photos of young girls and women. She had no idea.

They also found earrings he saved as trophies from those girls he had murdered, which connected their DNA to his possession. The detective labeled her photo as a survivor of Rodney Alcala, who remained on death row in San Quentin Prison, California, until he died in 2021 from natural causes.

> Blessed is the man who walketh not in
> the counsel of the ungodly, nor
> standeth in the way of sinners, nor
> sitteth in the seat of the scornful. But
> his delight is in the law of the Lord;
> and in his law doth he meditate day
> and night. And he shall be like a tree
> planted by the rivers of water, that
> bringeth forth his fruit in his season;
> his leaf also shall not wither; And
> whatsoever he doeth shall prosper.
> The ungodly are not so: but are like
> the chaff which the wind driveth
> away. Therefore the ungodly shall
> not stand in the judgment, nor
> sinners in the congregation of the
> righteous. For the Lord knoweth the

way of the righteous: but the way of
the ungodly shall perish.

— PSALM 1:1-6

He that dwelleth in the secret place of
the most High, shall abide under the
shadow of the Almighty. I will say of
the Lord, He is my refuge and my
fortress: my God; in him will I trust.

— PSALM 91:1-2

Thank God He spared her life because she listened to the Godly counsel of her sister. She did not hang out with the "Dating Game" serial killer.

Of course, her worried mother was praying for her on that trip. God answered her prayers.

She was able to follow her dreams, go to college, and graduate with her Fine Arts and Education degree. All praise be to God, she can live and tell her story today. Now forty years later, God still has a plan for her life to tell her story and give Him the glory.

CHAPTER 8
STEAL, KILL, AND DESTROY

A young college-aged single woman was driving her red Dodge Dart with hood scoops, black racing stripes, and mag wheels one evening with a new friend who wanted to have a get-together with a group of people to watch a Sonic game. When they arrived at his friend's apartment, there were no other people there yet.

Her friend asked to use her hotrod to go pick up some people and stop at the store for munchies. The game had started, so she wanted to watch it and stupidly said yes to the guy. He took her keys and car and drove off.

She waited alone with his friend, but she felt awkward about the situation. She was uncomfortable with this strange friend. Shockingly, he started forcing himself onto her and pushing her up against the wall. She struggled to get away from him successfully and ran out the door of the apartment.

It was dark outside in a heavily wooded location. She headed toward the main road where she knew she could walk to find a pay phone at a store. Once she got to the main road, she walked north and the opposite direction of traffic, but there were no cars on the road. She noticed what looked like a man's silhouette across the road on the other side also walking north in the darkness.

She got worried as he started rushing across the street over to her side of the road. She wanted to run, but again, there were no cars to flag down or jump out in front of, and there was nowhere to run. Sure enough, he rushed up behind her with a shiny chrome gun and pressed the nose of it into the middle of her back. He told her, "You will go where I tell you and do what I tell you to do."

As they were walking, he followed behind her, still pushing his gun on her back, which made her fearful of trying to get away. Still heading north on the main road, he told her to turn left at a corner street. There were homes and landscaping on only one side of the street as they turned the corner.

Then he told her to go into some dense bushes ahead at the corner house. That's when she lost control of her emotions and started sobbing and yelling her unfortunate story to him of why she was out there in the dark all alone.

"First, my friend stole my car tonight. Then his friend tried to rape me, but I got away through the woods. I just bought this white ski parka with the last of my money, and now you are doing this to me. No, I cannot do this!" she cried loudly.

Next, he told her to keep walking and not turn around, or he would shoot her. She continued walking past the houses in the dark and sobbing loudly out of control. After she passed by about five houses, she decided to turn around because she no longer felt his gun pressing against her back.

Miraculously he was gone! She ran to the closest house, rang the doorbell, and pounded on the door. She was yelling please help and call the police. The porch light came on, and an old man answered the door asking what was going on. She told him, "There is a man with a gun over there, but now he's gone. Someone stole my car and I need to call my brother to come and get me."

The old man told her to calm down, come inside, and offered her his phone. She made a call to her brother who came right away to pick her up and take her home. She learned some hard lessons. Her brother scolded her, "Do not hang out with strangers, never give your car keys to anyone, and pick better friends."

That morning, her mother came to ask her what she had been doing the previous night. She told her she was hanging out with some friends. Her mother told her oh no, you were doing more than that; tell the truth. She told her mother everything was just fine.

"No," her mother exclaimed, "I had to get up to pray for you in the night and something was going on. You're just not telling me because the Holy Spirit woke me up, and He was concerned for you in a life-and-death situation."

> For he shall give his angels charge over
>   thee, to keep thee in all thy ways.
>   They shall bear thee up in their
>   hands, lest thou dash thy foot
>   against a stone.
> Because he hath set his love upon me,
>   therefore will I deliver him:
> He shall call upon me, and I will answer
>   him: I will be with him in trouble; I
>   will deliver him, and honor him.
> With long life will I satisfy him, and
>   show him my salvation.

— PSALM 91:11-12; 14-16

> The thief cometh not, but for to steal,
>   and to kill, and to destroy: I am come

that they might have life, and that
they might have it more abundantly.

— JOHN 10:10

Once again, thank God for praying mothers who awake to the nudge of the Holy Spirit and heed the call to pray. The young lady was unharmed; she even got her car back with the help of her brother the next day.

She is blessed by God to be alive to talk about how the devil tried to steal, but he could not, and tried to kill, but he could not, and tried to destroy her, but he could not harm her in any way or even her new white ski parka. God's angels intervened because of her mother's prayer. He promises that He will deliver us from all our troubles. Surely, goodness, and mercy will follow us all the days of our lives. Halleluiah!

CHAPTER 9
HIP HEALING

There was a young married woman who had her second baby. It was a girl! God gave her the desire of her heart. As a girl, she wanted to get married and have a boy first and then a girl, and that's what God gave her. Only there was one problem, she could not stand up or walk after childbirth.

Doctors were unclear and told her she had soft tissue damage. They did not seem concerned about looking into the issue or doing X-rays. The hospital arranged a wheelchair service to transport her and sent her home in a wheelchair. Doctors explained she could not stand because the intensity of pain caused her body to collapse on the floor.

This was a game-changer. How does a young mother care for a newborn baby, let alone an active two-year-old boy, when she can't get out of bed? She could not even get to the bathroom. It was horrible that she had to use a bedpan. Her husband had to stay home from work to take care of the family, but things could not continue this way.

Finally, after two weeks at home in bed, her praying mother came over with her praying nurse friend from church. The nurse said that this is unheard of to not diagnose what is wrong or have follow-up appointments. They decided to pray the prayers of agreement together for healing and to stand on the promises of God's Word, that Jesus has already borne our griefs, sorrows, and pains, and by His stripes, we were healed.

All of them prayed in the Spirit in their heavenly language of tongues together. About fifteen minutes into their prayer time, something shifted in her hip area. She felt movement and heard a popping in her hip bones. She remembered the story about Jacob who wrestled with the angel. God touched his hip and changed his walk. Jacob's hip was out of joint, but that same God can put hips back into joint and that is exactly what He had done in that instant. The holy presence of God came into the room and swept all through her body and she felt heat flowing through her hip area.

Feeling the heavy love of God blanket over her, the young mom in tears explained what she was feeling to her mother and nurse friend. She knew God had heard and answered their prayers because she felt a hot fiery sensation in her hip area. Even Elijah called on the name of the Lord, and God answered by fire to demonstrate a miracle. They all began to praise God for a complete healing miracle.

They had strong, fervent, and unified prayer that touched the heart of God and He answered. The young mom was able to stand up for the first time in two weeks, and she began to take steps away from the bed. She was completely healed and praised God for His love, the miracle of healing, and His mercy.

> Again I say unto you, that if two of you
> shall agree on earth as touching any
> thing that they shall ask, it shall be
> done for them of my Father which is
> in heaven.
> For where two or three are gathered in
> my name, there am I in the midst of
> them.
>
> — MATTHEW 18:19-20 (KJVAE)

> He will regard the prayer of the desti-
> tute, and not despise their prayer.
>
> — PSALM 102:17 (KJVAE)

> But he was wounded for our transgres-
> sions, he was bruised for our iniqui-
> ties: the chastisement of our peace
> was upon him; and with his stripes
> we are healed.
>
> — ISAIAH 53:5 (KJVAE)

What would have happened to this young family if God did not heal this young mother's hip? Without God, there was a mother who could not provide care for her toddler or newborn baby.

Because God loves us, He wants us well and walking in wholeness, not broken or lacking anything. We must press into Him, hold on to and stand on His promises, believing His Word works. God is so faithful when anyone calls upon the name of Jesus, He will hear and answer their call and show them great and mighty things.

God heard the destitute prayer of the young mother, her mother, and her nurse friend as they gathered in His name and agreed in prayer. God answered according to the promises in His Word. Thank you, Jesus!

CHAPTER 10

TRANSPORTED

One year later, the young mother had her three-year-old son and a one-year-old daughter. It was clear that her husband was on drugs, and he was saying their marriage was over. It made no sense to her when he told her that he was taking their son and leaving, and she could have their daughter, whom she had just secured in her infant swing.

In confusion, she said no and wondered why he would say or do such a thing. He proceeded to grab their son, rushed him out to their 1970 Lincoln Station Wagon, and without taking time to fasten the toddler into his car seat, tossed him into the front seat. Then he quickly jumped in the driver's seat, locked the doors, and started the car.

The Mother followed him out of the house, witnessing this happening in front of her eyes. She rushed to the front of the car and threw her hands up in the air to plead with her husband to stop, but no, now the car lunged at her as she heard the engine rev up due to him accelerating the gas. He intended to run her down in the middle of the street in front of their house and their child!

In an instant, she suddenly found herself sitting on the curb across the street with her head in her hands, calling on God, and weeping with dread. She thought she had lost her son forever, but realized her life was saved by an angel in the split second. Next, she realized that she would need to call the police.

The police came and took the report that her husband kidnapped their son and attempted to run her down with their family wagon, and she explained how she was a living miracle because she was transported in a fraction of a second to the curb in a sitting position.

The cops found the husband with the son at a beach park called Golden Gardens and told him to take their child home. Fortunately, he did as they said, and they followed him home, where the mother was waiting and praying.

At the house, the mother insisted on taking both children to a safe place for the night. Still in the home, the police encouraged the dad to let the babies go with their mother. He'd put both the son and mother in harm's way.

The police assured him that the mother would keep the babies safe. And that they needed time for things to calm down and figure things out. The husband finally said yes to allowing the upset mother and children to leave together for the night.

Mother realized that her life was spared by the mercy of God, and His angels transported her rather than allowing her to be run down by the huge family wagon. Her husband was obviously on drugs, and it was time to fast and pray for direction. She figured out she needed to go get a Restraining Order and separate from her husband.

> And lead us not into temptation, but
> deliver us from evil: For thine is the
> kingdom, and the power, and the
> glory, for ever. Amen.
>
> — MATTHEW 6:13 (KJVAE)

> For he shall give his angels charge over
> thee, to keep thee in all thy ways.
> They shall bear thee up in their hands,
> lest thou dash thy foot against a
> stone.
>
> — PSALM 91:11-12 (KJVAE)

Too many times, women are caught up in life-threatening or abusive situations. Although there are resources available through the states to help in these circumstances, the church has advised women to stay and work things out with their abusive husbands.

God wants women to be smart and responsible, to protect themselves along with their children. There could have been different outcomes from this incident if God had not given His angels charge over her situation and intervened. These babies could have possibly ended up without a mother who was run down by a huge car and a father in jail for vehicular manslaughter.

Thank God He watches over His own. He is faithful to save us in the time of trouble and deliver us from evil, even death! Amen.

CHAPTER 11
GIFTS OPERATING IN CHURCH

A woman in her twenties was told by her doctor that she had arthritis in her hands and forearms. It was very painful at times. The doctor explained that it was because she had broken each of her wrists twice. There was nothing he could do about it, and the cold weather made it worse.

While living in Rancho Cucamonga, in sunny California, she visited her friend's church in Riverside. Toward the end of the service, the pastor called out people who had arthritis to raise their hands and come forward for prayer. The pastor said that he heard God say He was going to heal all those who had arthritis.

The young woman raised both hands and went forward for prayer. As she walked the aisle to the front, she felt the presence of Father God touch her hands and forearms and they began to tingle. She felt the arthritis go out and leave her body. She was healed, pain-free, and full of joy knowing the love of God changed her life with a miracle.

> For to one is given by the Spirit the word
>> of wisdom; to another the word of
>> knowledge by the same Spirit; to
>> another faith by the same Spirit; to
>> another the gifts of healing by the
>> same Spirit; to another the working
>> of miracles; to another prophecy; to
>> another discerning of spirits; to
>> another divers kinds of tongues; to
>> another the interpretation of
>> tongues:
>
>> — 1 CORINTHIANS 12:8-10
>>> (KJVAE)

With this word of knowledge, the pastor called out the people with arthritis and initiated the gift of healing. Through God's healing miracles, He changes lives forever. This lady's quality of life improved along with her capabilities. If we only knew how much God loves us, we would believe for more. He's a good, gracious God!

CHAPTER 12
SHOCKING EVENTS

There was a young mother, Sally. She had a boy who was 3 and a girl who was 1. She had temporary custody of her children and a restraining order. Because the father was abusive and on drugs, his mother had agreed to supervise visits for the children.

When the father and his mother came to pick up the children in her car, Sally felt something was off. So, she quickly walked to the corner to look down the street. She witnessed the grandmother help the father take the children and their car seats from her car and put them into his.

She drove off alone, and shortly after, the father drove off with the children.

When she was giving the children their evening baths, she noticed an injury or sore spot on the boy's private parts. It was discovered that the father was sexually abusing her children when the boy told her what his daddy did to him.

In shock, Sally called the police right away. They came promptly and interviewed the boy that evening. The next morning, the Child Protective Services caseworker came to the home; he also interviewed the boy. The boy was consistent in his descriptive details of the abuse.

The mother was sent to Harbor View Medical Center where both children would be examined, interviewed, and photographed for injuries.

She tried to keep it together, but she was so grief-stricken and thought she was having a mental breakdown. Her boy was interviewed for the fourth time by the police from a different city from where the father's brother resided, and the uncle was named as one of the perpetrators in the child abuse case.

The Child Protection Services caseworker told the mother not to allow the father or his brother to have any more contact with the children, or she could lose custody of them. This was a no-brainer to her. She was worried sick emotionally, physically, and mentally already for the well-being of her children.

The young mother had moved away so the father could not find them. The police and Child Protection caseworker both informed the father and his brother that they were being criminally investigated and should not expect to see the children until the courts ruled.

In the night, the mother heard familiar voices outside of her new apartment. It was the father and his brother. They were knocking on her neighbors' doors asking if they had seen a little boy and girl that had been kidnapped by their mother. She found out the next day they were showing pictures to the neighbors, trying to find her little ones, and accusing her of what they were intending to do, kidnap the children.

While their belongings were still in boxes, they moved to another location the following day. It was apparent that the father would use any means to save himself from being prosecuted, even if it meant kidnapping the witness, the children. The mother decided they would have to hide out from public places. There could be no more time spent at the parks and no playing outside. It was obvious the children were at risk and not safe, so she would have to always look over her shoulder and be aware of their surroundings.

The mother had no attorney, but the father hired three for himself. They brought a motion to the court every week, it seemed. The initial divorce was expunged because his attorneys lied to say the couple had properties to divide, but there was absolutely none. They only had their cars.

The children and the mother were court-ordered to start therapy and counseling, and the boy was court-ordered to undergo a psychological evaluation. However, the judge also ordered the father to undergo psych evaluations as well as drug testing. A year later, through fasting and answers to prayers, God sent the mother an attorney pro bono just in time before the two-week trial.

Discovery led to evidence of injury and showed consistent testimonials of the son. Expert witnesses were all in favor of the children being protected from the father. The mother was awarded sole care, custody, and control of the children, as well as a full restraining order for all of them.

The father's drug and alcohol testing revealed all positive tests. Consequently, he was court-ordered to enroll in a detox program as well as attend Alcoholics Anonymous. Additionally, the judge ordered him to attend anger management classes based on his revealed violent behavior episodes petitioned for in the restraining order.

He was also court-ordered to get family counseling, psychotherapy, and sexual deviancy therapy due to the discovery by police, Child Protection Services caseworker, and medical workers. He was granted no visitation and no supervised visitation either. God changed it from the disengaged grandmother not supervising visits to zero visits.

The father was court-ordered to pay his three attorneys and the mother's attorney. The Dissolution of Marriage was final after waiting through court motions and the court-ordered appointments for another 18 months including a trial.

With decree in hand, the mother wanted to flee the mess and stigma it would bring upon her children. They needed healing and a fresh start. Although there were many moves to new residences during the court battles, the mother still worried the children would be kidnapped by their father or someone he hired to do the job. She never felt safe again because there was a criminal case pending against the father and his brother.

Counseling had been in place for six months. It only served to cause pain by reopening the wounded hearts, injured thoughts, violated minds, and terrorized emotions of her little ones. There was no relief for the innocent children who had to relive and rehash the abuse they had undergone. The mother believed this counseling was contrary to Biblical principles, which would allow her children's horrific experiences to be healed, forgiven, and forgotten. Her prayer was that God would erase her children's memories of abuse and heal their wounds of the past.

The mother and her children were all given new wardrobes from a missionary friend who was a recipient of sample designer clothing for a Nordstrom buyer. There was an abundance of new clothing that was dressy, sporty, and gorgeous. This was symbolic of the way that God would give them His covering and hide them from the enemy. Years ago, these high-quality clothes would have been worth thousands of dollars.

The Bible says, God will supply all our needs and that He most certainly did. He also covered them with His divine protection to hide them from further kidnapping attempts. God made a way of escape that they were able to bear.

After much prayer and fasting, the young mother waited months for the Lord to show her when to leave the state. By now, she had moved 15 times in two years and her essentials were packed and she was ready and free with her decree to leave at any time.

In the middle of the night, she awoke to the tune of a song and a new word she did not know. She called her mother to see if she knew the word and she did. It was a native name of a southern border town called Toppenish, and the tune in her heart was to the song "Edelweiss" from a movie called *The Sound of Music*. In the movie, the Trap family were planning to leave their homeland to escape Nazi Germany in the darkness of the night.

The Spirit of God had quickened her to get up and get the children in the car after talking to her mother on the phone. She was already prepared to leave her homeland, family, and lifelong friends. Finally, the moment she was waiting on God for was happening. She knew the route to drive to exit the state in the darkness of the night, like the Trap family who safely escaped from their enemies.

The mother knew in her heart for sure that the time had arrived for her to be delivered from the abusive, stressful, and insecure life with her children in her custody. The Holy Spirit was present in guiding their path into a new life, secure in Christ, just the way Abraham also left his family, friends, and homeland to start over.

> God is my strength and power; and he
> maketh my way perfect.
>
> — 2 SAMUEL 22:33 (KJVAE)

> Let us break their bands asunder, and
> cast away their cords from us.
>
> — PSALM 2:3 (KJVAE)

> the Lord will deliver him in time of
>   trouble.
>
>   — PSALM 41:1B (KJVAE)

> Call unto me, and I will answer thee,
>   and show thee great and mighty
>   things, which thou knowest not.
>
>   — JEREMIAH 33:3 (KJVAE)

God always makes a way if there seems to be no way. God told Abram in Genesis 12 to get out of his land, leave his relatives, and go to the land He would show him. Abram obeyed God. Sally obeyed God too.

As a cautious mother, she was watchful of her surroundings for years to come. She changed their names, put the children in private schools, and raised them in church with Christian friends. They never went without food, clothing, or shelter. Just as God provided expensive Nordstrom clothing, He was their covering and a high tower of refuge.

CHAPTER 13
MIGRAINES GONE

During a Bible convention in Arizona, at Christ for the Nations Church, a speaker said angels were present to heal people and that miracles were going to break out everywhere in the meeting.

People with weight problems miraculously lost weight. People with teeth problems were healed and received fillings in their teeth. Also, God healed people with back problems. One person who could not bend down due to metal in her back from surgery was able to do the impossible: bend over to touch the floor! All the people who suffered from migraine headaches were asked to raise their hands for healing and that God would touch them right where they were.

A lady who suffered from debilitating migraines that put her life on hold at times lifted her hands to receive a miracle. There were times she had to miss work from being so sick. Although she was fine in the meeting, she believed God could heal her from having any more migraines.

She felt a sharp pain in her little toe that she had previously broken. It was bad and had been set back in place from a perpendicular position to her foot with emergency room services only a few months ago. It was not perfectly placed with its neighboring toe; it had a little gap.

When she looked down at her little toe, it was perfectly relocated into its original spot where it was initially touching the other toes before the injury. She realized that God was showing her He cared about her condition from head to toe. He supernaturally moved her displaced toe during the moment of sharp pain. Now there was no pain, just a perfectly placed little toe.

That is when the presence of God and His love gushed through her entire being and she began to cry. God had her attention, He told her, "I healed your toe and put it in its original position rather than where the doctors placed it with a gap. I gave you this as a sign to show you that I healed your migraines too. My daughter, you are healed from head to toe."

God's love, power, and presence were so strong on her that she could hardly talk without crying. However, she was able to share the miracle with her mother who was attending the convention with her and others around her. When the meeting was dismissed, many other testimonies of miracle healings had occurred.

> "If you will diligently listen and pay
> attention to the voice of the Lord
> your God, and do what is right in
> His sight, and listen to His
> commandments, and keep[foremost
> in your thoughts and actively obey]
> all His precepts and statutes, then I
> will not put on you any of the
> diseases which I have put on the
> Egyptians; for I am the Lord who
> heals you."
>
> — EXODUS 15:26 (AMP)

> And He went throughout all Galilee,
> teaching in their synagogues and
> preaching the good news (gospel) of
> the kingdom, and healing every kind
> of disease and every kind of sickness
> among the people[demonstrating
> and revealing that He was indeed
> the promised Messiah].
>
> — MATTHEW 4:23 (AMP)

> I assure you and most solemnly say to
> you, anyone who believes in Me [as
> Savior] will also do the things that I
> do; and he will do even greater
> things than these [in extent and
> outreach], because I am going to the
> Father. And I will do whatever you
> ask in My name [as My representa-
> tive], this I will do, so that the Father
> may be glorified and celebrated in
> the Son. If you ask Me anything in
> My name [as My representative], I
> will do it.
>
> — JOHN 14:12-14 (AMP)

Doctors are unable to cure migraine headaches. They can treat the symptoms and that's about all they can do. People are known to suffer for years and miss out on life events and meaningful times with their family and friends. Migraines have a way of stealing one's health, days, and life. Does this sound familiar to the role of the devil who comes to steal, kill, and destroy?

When someone is healed of migraines, it is life-changing, resulting in transformation into a new blessed life. One who is healed no longer suffers, misses work, loses pay, or misses out on family or church events.

God is so faithful to provide healing miracles when we press into Him. Stay in faith and believe in the Word. He takes our suffering away. Amen!

CHAPTER 14
DIVORCE OF A CHRISTIAN

The same lady who was healed of migraines in the last story had been in an abusive marriage. When she broke her little toe on the couch leg, her husband refused to take her to the ER. She could not walk or drive.

She waited for hours until her 16-year-old daughter got home from work that night to drive her to the hospital. It was difficult for her to heal completely because she was on her feet all the time teaching.

Her daughter and twin brother convinced her to leave their abusive father. They witnessed his disruptive, abusive behavior in the home toward her and them. Her migraines were most likely due to stress and emotional and verbal abuse. God told her one day, "I gave you a brain; you have to choose to use it."

She started praying and fasting for a way of escape. Praying for him all these years hadn't changed his free will to be abusive. When reading Mark 10, verse 9, the Spirit gave her an understanding that firstly, God did not even put her and the husband together; she was deceived and unequally yoked. Secondly, He does not expect her to stay with someone abusive.

It turns out that the husband was trying to refinance the home, but there was a Thanksgiving holiday in the count for 5 days, causing the refi to fall through. Consequently, they lost the home with a notice to vacate in 3 days. She knew this was God's answer. Although he was distraught over it, she rejoiced in her heart to be delivered from him no matter what the cost. He soon filed for a divorce. Now no house tied them together or needed to be divided, which made a divorce easier.

> What therefore God hath joined
> together, let no man put asunder.

> — MARK 10:9 (KJVAE)

> Be ye not unequally yoked together with
> unbelievers: for what fellowship
> hath righteousness with unright-
> eousness? and what communion
> hath light with darkness?

> — 2 CORINTHIANS 6:14 (KJVAE)

> Verily I say unto you, Whatsoever ye
>   shall bind on earth shall be bound
>   in heaven; and whatsoever ye shall
>   loose on earth shall be loosed in
>   heaven.

— MATTHEW 18:18 (KJVAE)

God did not join this couple together, but God was the one who drove the husband out of the house by allowing the loan to go into default. The woman was loosed from the bondage of an unequally yoked marriage. Even after praying for many years for the husband to get sincere with God, things only got worse. Despite circumstances, God's love prevailed so she and her children could live in peace.

It's never "The End" of our God's interventions; we have eternity in Christ. Hold on to and believe in your miracles by continually thanking God for the promises in His Word. Remember, the devil has been defeated and disarmed by your testimonies.

> And they overcame him by the blood of
>   the Lamb, and by the word of their
>   testimony; and they loved not their
>   lives unto the death.

— REV.12:11 (KJVAE)

This passage richly tells us to abide in His Word and His love, produce fruit that will remain, and that the Father will give you whatever you ask in Jesus's name. This will engage you with His everlasting promises that you can believe and receive.

God bless you as you walk in miracles and divine protection!

AFTERWORD

PRAYER OF SALVATION

> For God so loved the world, that he gave
> his only begotten Son, that whoso-
> ever believeth in him should not
> perish, but have everlasting life.
> For God sent not his Son into the world
> to condemn the world; but that the
> world through him might be saved.

> — JOHN 3:16-17

Do you know where you would spend eternity? Does Christ live in you? If you are not sure where you will go when you die and you want to know for sure, then please say this "prayer of salvation" aloud to God in heaven.

Dear Heavenly Father,

Come into my heart. Thank You for sending Jesus to die on the cross for my sins. Thank You, Jesus, that You rose again on the third day, and You overcame sin, death, and the grave for me. Forgive my sins and wash my heart clean with Your redeeming blood. Make me a new creature in Christ and receive me into the family of God to live eternally with You. I surrender my life to You and ask You to fill me with Your Holy Spirit so I may walk in divine protection. Guide me in Your ways of truth for the rest of my life. I choose to serve You, the one and only true God, giver of life eternal.

Amen!

Welcome to the family of our Creator God, who hears and answers our prayers.

PRAYER TO BE BAPTIZED IN THE HOLY SPIRIT

> For John truly baptized with water; but
> ye shall be baptized with the Holy
> Ghost not many days hence.
> And they were all filled with the Holy
> Ghost, and began to speak with
> other tongues, as the Spirit gave
> them utterance.
>
> — ACTS 1:5 AND 2:4

Do you want to be empowered by and infilled with the Spirit of God to walk in the gifts of the Spirit now? Ask God to baptize you in the Holy Ghost by saying this prayer aloud.

Dear Father in Heaven,

I ask in Jesus' name that You fill me with Your Holy Spirit and power, baptize me as You did Your people in Ephesians 5. Pour out Your Spirit upon me with the evidence of speaking a new heavenly language.

Thank You for Your Word that tells me You hear my prayer even before I call on you. Your Word also says, whatever I ask for in Jesus' name, You will do it. I ask in Jesus' name open the eyes and ears of my heart to see and hear what the Spirit is showing and telling me. Cause me to walk in miracles and Your divine protection. Reveal the mysteries and understanding of Your Word to me through the Holy Spirit.

Amen!

Welcome to the blessed life!

A WHOLE NEW BLESSED LIFE

> But his delight is in the law of the Lord,
>   And on His law [His precepts and
>   teachings] he [habitually] meditates
>   day and night.
> And he will be like a tree firmly planted
>   [and fed] by streams of water, which
>   yields its fruit in its season; its leaf
>   does not wither; And in whatever he
>   does, he prospers [and comes to
>   maturity].
>
> — PSALM 1:2-3 (AMP)

Welcome to the new blessed life in Christ. As a child growing up in church, we sang a song, "Read your Bible Pray Every Day." We learned that the Bible is food and living water to our Spirit man. As we grow in God, He makes the Bible come alive and reveals all things to our understanding while His Word nourishes us. It is important to read the Bible and pray every day so God can teach us through the Holy Spirit, who lives in us.

It is an exciting and good life when we press into God. He shines His light on us and lights up our paths in life to direct us to the right places He would have us go. It is essential to attend church where we sense the presence of God. If He is not there, then find a church where God is moving by His Spirit. God is faithful to bring the right people into our lives and take out the wrong ones when we follow Him.

God bless you in your new walk with Him!

ABOUT THE AUTHOR

From a tender age, Sally's spiritual journey was colored by profound experiences of faith and divine encounters. Raised in a devout Christian home, she invited Jesus into her heart as a young child, setting her on a path of unwavering faith. Sally's early introduction to the power of prayer and the Holy Spirit at Philadelphia Church in Seattle nurtured a deep-seated belief in the miraculous and the importance of spiritual gifts.

Sally's educational journey mirrored her spiritual quest, overcoming learning challenges through prayer and perseverance to achieve academic success. Earning a Bachelor's Degree in Art Education from Seattle Pacific University and a Master's Degree in Education from Azusa Pacific University, Sally's career as an educator was supported by a philosophy that "All things are possible," a belief that she instilled in her students over thirty years of teaching.

Ordained through the Morris Cerullo School of Ministry, Sally's commitment to spreading the gospel took a new turn when she and her husband, Eric, felt called to share their faith through "Eric and Sally Crosstalk," a forthcoming series of engagements and digital content aimed at inspiring others with messages of hope, faith, and divine intervention.

Sally's authorial voice is a testament to her life's miracles, chronicled in her book *Miracles and Divine Protection*. Here, she shares not only her personal experiences of healing and divine protection but also the universal promise that God's grace and power are accessible to all who receive Him. Through her writings, Sally aspires to encourage others to seek a life-changing relationship with God through Jesus, believing firmly that what God has done for her, He can do for anyone.

As Sally prepares to expand her ministry alongside Eric, her story continues as a beacon of God's power to regenerate lives, inviting readers to explore the depths of a life lived in close communion with God.

Website: EScrosstalk.com
Email: ericandsally4@gmail.com

facebook.com/ESCROSSTALK
x.com/EricandSal20358
youtube.com/EricandSallyCrosstalk

www.ingramcontent.com/pod-product-compliance
Lightning Source LLC
La Vergne TN
LVHW041233080426
835508LV00011B/1183